W9-BQU-442

to: _____

from: _____

Published by Hallmark Books,
a division of Hallmark Cards, Inc.,
Kansas City, MO 64141
Visit us on the Web at Hallmark.com.

Editorial Director: Todd Hafer
Editor: Theresa Trinder
Art Director: Kevin Swanson
Designer: Mary Eakin
Production Artist: Dan Horton
Hand Lettering: Sarah Cole

ISBN: 978-1-59530-184-0
BOK4353
Printed and bound in China

baby steps

A LITTLE HANDBOOK FOR HAPPY PARENTING

WRITTEN BY
Dee Ann Stewart

ILLUSTRATED BY
Ralanna Forbis & Ivan Chan

♥

"twinkle, twinkle,
little star.
how i wonder
what you are."

JANE TAYLOR

DON'T BASE YOUR
PARENTING SKILLS
ON YOUR ABILITY
TO KEEP A HAT ON
YOUR CHILD.

THE FIRST SIGN OF THE
"I'M POOPING!" FACE
IS A GOOD TIME
TO PASS THE BABY
TO SOMEONE ELSE.

YES, THE BABY
WILL DRESS BETTER
THAN YOU FOR AWHILE.

TRY NOT TO BE JEALOUS.

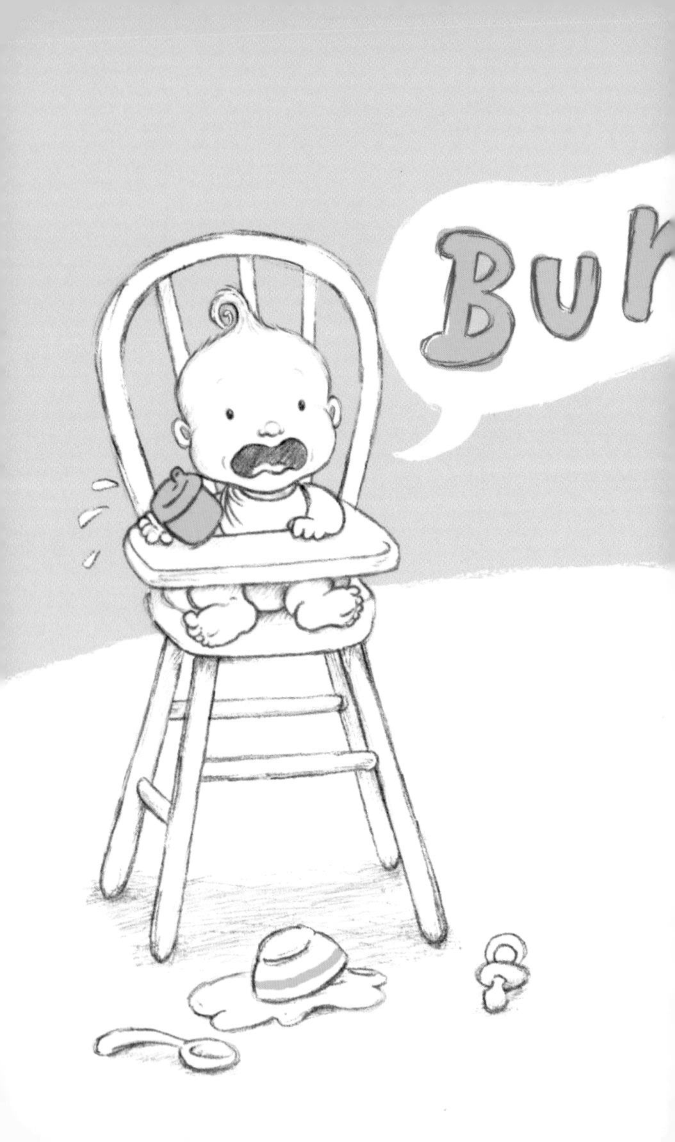
Bur

-rrrp!

YOU'LL CLAP AND CHEER
WHEN THEY BURP.
EVENTUALLY YOU'LL WANT
TO BREAK THIS HABIT.

A LOT OF
DADS-TO-BE
ALSO EAT FOR TWO.

BOTTLE FEEDING,
LIKE OUTSOURCING,
CAN BE A GOOD
EXECUTIVE DECISION.

YOUR BABY MAY TAKE
"no-leak protection"

AS A PERSONAL CHALLENGE.

A BABY'S DESIRE
TO BE NAKED IS
ONLY AN ISSUE IF IT
LASTS INTO HER TEENS.

BATH TIME IS SUCCESSFUL
WHEN THE KID GETS
WETTER THAN YOU DO.

IT WON'T MATTER THAT
YOU CAN'T GET OUT MUCH.

BABIES PROVIDE
HOURS and HOURS OF
FREE ENTERTAINMENT.

CHILDREN WHO GET UP
BEFORE SUNRISE
NEED LOVE, TOO.

yes, teething is bad.
and it actually
leads to real, live
teeth they can
use to bite stuff.

THE ONLY BABY FOOD
YOU SHOULD SAMPLE
IS THE FRUIT.

SERIOUSLY, ONLY THE FRUIT.

WHEN THEY MEET YOU
AT THE BEDROOM DOOR,
IT'S TIME TO
GET RID OF THE CRIB.

THERE'S A REASON
THEY CALL IT
A POWER NAP.

IF A KID GETS
HIS HANDS ON
YOUR CELL PHONE,
HE'LL PROBABLY CALL
SOMEONE YOU KNOW.

rule no. 17

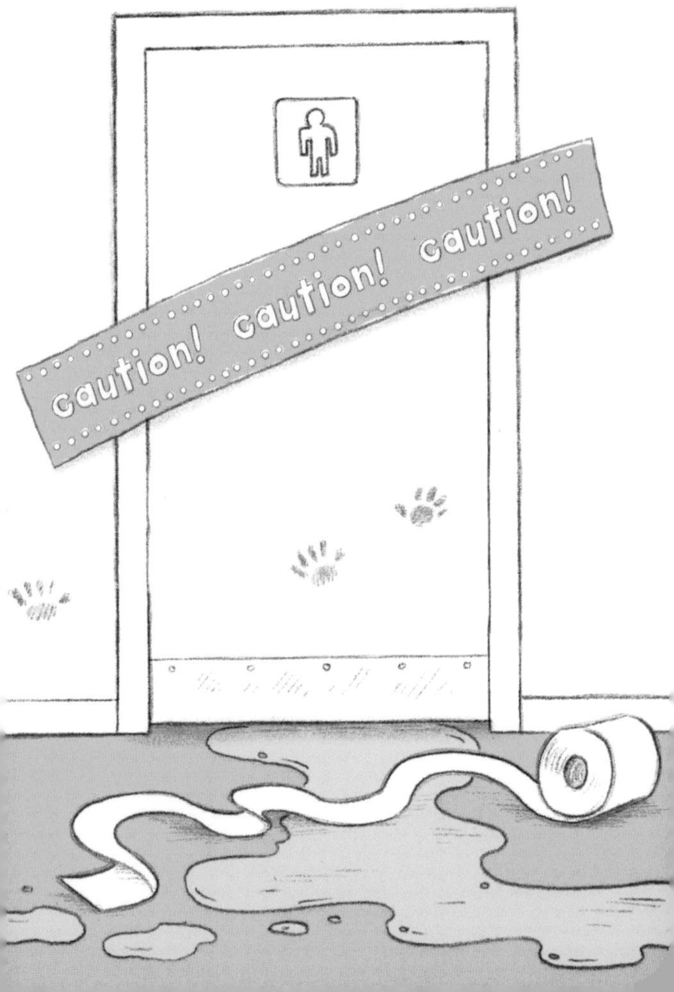

REMEMBER, OTHER
PARENTS WILL ALWAYS
SEEM COOLER THAN YOU.

THERE ARE
NO BLUEPRINTS FOR
HOMEMADE FORTS.

RUNNING THROUGH
THE SPRINKLER
COUNTS AS SWIMMING
IF YOUR CHILD
IS YOUNG ENOUGH.

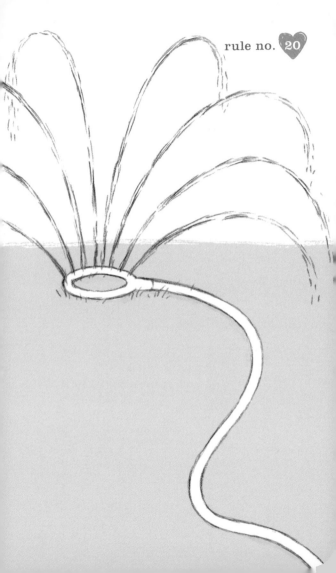

THERE'S NOT MUCH
YOU CAN DO ABOUT IT.

HOTEL BEDS ARE MADE
FOR JUMPING ON.

IF ONLY THE
CLEANING UP WERE
HALF AS FUN

AS THE MESSING UP.

iF YOU GiVe a BOY
CLOTHeS aS a GiFT,
He'LL WONDeR
WHaT He DiD WRONG.

DON'T BASE YOUR
CHILD'S ATHLETIC CAREER
ON THE FIRST DAY
OF SOCCER PRACTICE.

IN FACT,
DON'T BASE ANYTHING
ON THE FIRST DAY
OF SOCCER PRACTICE.

THE PLACE YOU
SEND THEM FOR A
TIME-OUT SHOULDN'T
BE TOO MUCH FUN.

THE MINUTE A
TOY GETS DONATED
TO CHARITY

is the minute it becomes their favorite.

THE KEY TO A GOOD
BIRTHDAY PARTY
IS MAKING SURE
THE PARENTS TAKE
THE RIGHT KIDS HOME.

DESCRIBING BROCCOLI
AS A CUTE LITTLE TREE
DOESN'T MEAN THEY'LL
EAT IT.

WHY, OH, WHY DO THEY
GiVE KiDS COMBS
On SCHOOL PicTURE DAY?

NEVER UNDERESTIMATE
THE POWER OF A BRIBE.

one day, all their
pants are three
inches too short.

IT Happens
JUST Like THAT.

GRANDMAS ARE
GREAT BABYSITTERS,
AND THEY'RE LESS LIKELY
TO SNEAK BOYS OVER.

RESIST THE URGE
TO WAVE TO A CHILD
WHO'S SWINGING.

SHE WILL WANT
TO WAVE BACK.

THEY CALL IT THE
GREAT OUTDOORS
BECAUSE IT'S FREE.

IF YOU'RE NOT
ABSOLUTELY POSITIVE
YOU'RE GOING
TO THE ZOO,
DON'T TELL THEM
YOU'RE GOING
TO THE ZOO!

IT'S OKAY TO SEND THEM
TO DANCE CLASS JUST
SO YOU CAN POINT OUT
WHICH ONE'S YOURS.

GET USED TO
LOTS AND LOTS
OF QUESTIONS THAT
BEGIN WITH "WHY?"

EVERY CHILD THINKS
SHE INVENTED THE
KNOCK-KNOCK JOKE.

THE FIRST FIVE HUNDRED
MAY BE PRETTY FUNNY.

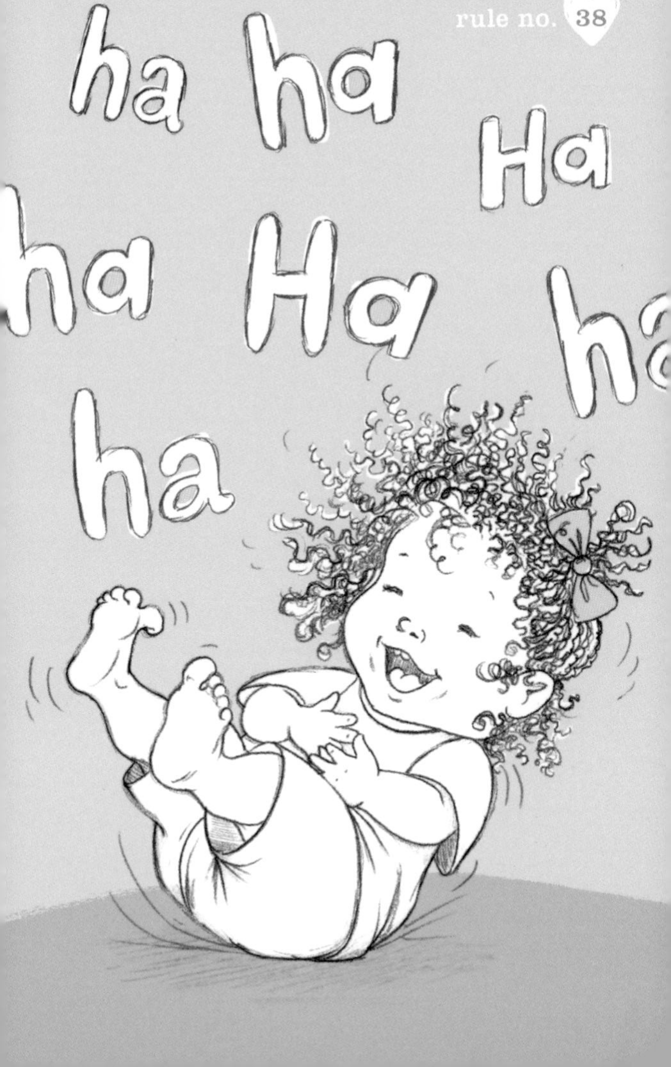
ha ha
Ha
ha Ha
ha
ha

NOTHING WEIGHS MORE
THAN A CHILD WHO HAS
FALLEN ASLEEP IN THE CAR
ON THE WAY HOME.

AND NOTHING
FEELS BETTER THAN
BEING THERE FOR THEM
AT THE BOTTOM
OF THE SLIDE. OR JUST
ABOUT ANYWHERE.

♥

"EVERY CHILD BEGINS
THE WORLD AGAIN."

THOREAU

If you have enjoyed this book
or it has touched your life in some way,
we would love to hear from you.

Please send your comments to:
Hallmark Book Feedback
P.O. Box 419034
Mail Drop 215
Kansas City, MO 64141

Or e-mail us at: booknotes@hallmark.com